P9-CZV-260

JANICE VANCLEAVE'S
WILD, WACKY, AND WEIRD
SCIENCE EXPERIMENTS

JANICE VANCLEAVE'S
WILD, WACKY, AND WEIRD
ASTRONOMY EXPERIMENTS

ROSEN
PUBLISHING

NEW YORK

This edition published in 2017 by:
The Rosen Publishing Group, Inc.
29 East 21st Street
New York, NY 10010

Library of Congress Cataloging-in-Publication Data

Names: VanCleave, Janice Pratt, author.
Title: Janice VanCleave's wild, wacky, and weird astronomy experiments / Janice VanCleave.
Other titles: Wild, wacky, and weird astronomy experiments
Description : New York : Rosen Central, 2017. | Series: Janice Vancleave's wild, wacky, and weird science experiments | Includes bibliographical references and index.
Identifiers: ISBN 9781477789636 (library bound) | ISBN 9781477789612 (pbk.) | ISBN 9781477789629 (6-pack)
Subjects: LCSH: Astronomy—Experiments—Juvenile literature. | Science projects—Juvenile literature.
Classification: LCC QB46.V364 2016 | DDC 520.78—dc23

Manufactured in China

Experiments first published in *Janice VanCleave's 202 Oozing, Bubbling, Dripping, and Bouncing Experiments* by John Wiley & Sons, Inc. copyright © 1996 Janice VanCleave.

CONTENTS

INTRODUCTION

Astronomy is the study of the planets, the stars, and other bodies in space. Since the beginning of humankind, people have looked to the heavens to try to understand the stars, the planets, and our sun. In modern times, we have rocketed into space to land on the moon. We have built an International Space Station to do research in space and powerful telescopes to peer at the far reaches of the universe.

The people who choose astronomy as a career do a variety of work. Some scientists study the planets and others study galaxies. Some astronomers work to learn more about black holes and the universe. Solar scientists focus on our sun, the star that enables life to exist on the earth. All these people have something in common: They are constantly asking questions to learn even more about space.

This book is a collection of science experiments about astronomy. What happens during a solar eclipse? Why does the moon shine? What causes Saturn's rings? You will find the answers to these and many other questions by doing the experiments in this book.

HOW TO USE THIS BOOK

Before you get started, be sure to read each experiment completely before starting. The following sections are included for all the experiments.

» **PURPOSE:** *The basic goals for the experiment.*

» **MATERIALS:** *A list of supplies you will need.*
You will experience less frustration and more fun if you gather all the necessary materials for the experiments before you begin. You lose your train of thought when you have to shop and search for supplies.

» **PROCEDURE:** *Step-by-step instructions on how to perform the experiment.*
Follow each step very carefully, never skip steps, and do not add your own. **Safety is of the utmost importance, and by reading the experiment before starting, then following the instructions exactly, you can feel confident that no unexpected results will occur. Ask an adult to help you when you are working with anything sharp or hot. If adult supervisor is required, it will be noted in the experiment.**

» **RESULTS:** *An explanation stating exactly what is expected to happen.*
This is an immediate learning tool. If the expected results are achieved, you will know that you did the experiment correctly. If your results are

not the same as described in the experiment, carefully read the instructions and start over from the first step.

» **WHY?** *An explanation of why the results were achieved.*
You will be rewarded with successful experiments if you read each experiment carefully, follow the steps in order, and do not substitute materials.

THE SCIENTIFIC METHOD

Scientists identify a problem or observe an event. Then they seek solutions or explanations through research and experimentation. By doing the experiments in this book, you will learn to follow experimental steps and make observations. You will also learn many scientific principles that have to do with astronomy.

In the process, the things you see or learn may lead you to new questions. For example, perhaps you have completed the experiment that looks at splatter to determine why moon craters are spread out. Now you wonder what would happen if you dropped each pebble from different heights. That's great! Every scientist is curious and asks new questions about what they learn. When you design a new experiment, it is a good idea to follow the scientific method.

1. Ask a question.

2. Do some research about your question. What do you already know?

3. Come up with a hypothesis, or a possible answer to your question.

4. Design an experiment to test your hypothesis. Make sure the experiment is repeatable.

5. Collect the data and make observations.

6. Analyze your results.

7. Reach a conclusion. Did your results support your hypothesis?

Many times the experiment leads to more questions and a new experiment.

Always remember that when devising your own science experiment, have a knowledgeable adult review it with you before trying it out. Ask them to supervise it as well.

BENT

PURPOSE To demonstrate how the thickness of an atmosphere affects how light is bent.

MATERIALS modeling clay   2 shiny pennies
           2 drinking cups   tap water

PROCEDURE

1. Stick a grape-sized piece of clay inside the bottom of each cup.

2. Press a penny in each piece of clay so that it is in the very center of the cup.

3. Fill one cup with water.

4. Place both cups on the edge of a table. The cups must be side by side and even with the edge of the table.

5. Stand close to the table. Then, take a few steps backward while observing the pennies in the cups.

6. Stop when you can no longer see either of the pennies.

RESULTS The ·penny in the cup filled with air disappears from view first, while you can still see the penny in the cup filled with water.

WHY? You see the penny in the water at a greater distance because light enters the cup, reflects from the penny, hits the surface of the water, and is **refracted** (bent) toward your eye. The water is thicker than the air and thicker materials refract the light more. A change in the thickness

8

of the earth's atmosphere (the gases around a planet) due to pollution, increases the refraction of light. Venus' thick atmosphere refracts light much more than does the earth's atmosphere. An observer on Venus would see many **mirages** (optical illusions due to atmospheric conditions) and distortions because of this.

HEAT SHIELD

PURPOSE To determine how space acts as a heat shield.

MATERIALS quart (liter) wide-mouthed glass jar with a lid
warm tap water
2 thermometers
thermos
2 drinking cups
timer

PROCEDURE

1. Fill the jar with warm tap water.

2. Place one of the thermometers in the jar for 2 minutes.

3. Read and record the temperature of the water.

4. Pour half of the water from the jar into the thermos, then close the lids on the thermos and the jar.

5. Allow the thermos and the jar to sit undisturbed for 1 hour.

6. Open the jar and the thermos. Fill one of the cups with water from the thermos and fill the second cup with water from the jar.

7. Place one thermometer in each of the cups.

8. Wait 1 minute, then read and record the temperature of the water in each cup.

RESULTS The temperature of the water inside the thermos changes less than does the temperature of the water inside the glass jar.

WHY? Between the inside and outside of the thermos is a partial vacuum (space with nothing in it). Heat has difficulty traveling through a vacuum; thus, the vacuum acts as a heat shield. The partial vacuum separating celestial (of the heavens or sky) bodies is called space. Materials that allow heat to move through them are called conductors. Like the partial vacuum in the thermos, space is a poor conductor. Thus space acts as a shield, protecting celestial bodies from solar heat.

Heat Shield

RINGS

PURPOSE To determine what causes Saturn's rings.

MATERIALS 3 sharpened pencils
masking tape
drawing compass
stiff cardboard, such as the back of a writing tablet
scissors
cookie sheet
salt
adult helper

PROCEDURE

1. Tape two of the pencils together so that their points are even.

2. Use the compass to draw a circle with an 8-inch (20-cm) diameter (length of a straight line passing through the center of the circle with both endpoints on the circle) on the cardboard.

3. Cut out the circle and have an adult use the point of the compass to punch a hole in the center.

4. Place the circle of cardboard, with the rough side of the hole down, on the cookie sheet.

5. Evenly cover the surface of the cardboard with salt.

6. Ask your helper to stand the third pencil point-down in the hole in the cardboard circle.

7. Rest the points of the taped pencils against the cardboard as your helper spins the cardboard around one full turn.

RESULTS As your helper turns the cardboard circle, the pencil points push the salt to the side, forming two cleared paths.

WHY? Saturn's rings are made of icy particles. Just as the pencil points move through the salt crystals in this experiment, astronomers believe that Saturn's moons move through the icy particles, pushing them into separate bands. These moons are called shepherd satellites (a small body that revolves around a larger body). The moons are given this name because they herd the icy particles in the rings.

FARTHEST

PURPOSE To demonstrate how Neptune sometimes becomes the outermost orbital body.

MATERIALS scissors
ruler
string
sheet of paper
6 pushpins
pencil
bulletin board (thick cardboard will work)

PROCEDURE

1. Cut a 12-inch (30-cm) piece of string and tie the ends together to form a loop.

2. Secure the paper to the bulletin board with four of the pushpins.

3. In the middle of the paper, draw a line ½ inch (1.25 cm) shorter than the length of the loop and stick a pushpin into the bulletin board at each end of the line. Loop the string around the pushpins.

4. Place the pencil so that its point is inside the loop.

5. Keep the string taut as you guide the pencil around the inside of the string to draw an ellipse (oval) on the paper.

6. Cut a second piece of string 8 inches (20 cm) long.

7. Repeat steps 1 through 5 with the 8-inch (20-cm) string to draw a smaller ellipse inside the larger one.

8. Move the pushpins until you can draw a small ellipse inside the larger one with one end of the small ellipse overlapping the larger one.

RESULTS Two overlapping ellipses are drawn.

WHY? The orbit (path of an object around another body) of each planet (or planetoid) has an elliptical shape. Pluto's orbit, represented by the longer string, is usually the outermost in the solar system. During its journey around the sun, however, Pluto moves inside Neptune's orbit for a period of time, making Neptune's orbit the outermost. The two bodies do not collide, because Pluto's orbit is above Neptune's.

IN PLACE

PURPOSE To demonstrate the point of balance between the earth and the moon.

MATERIALS drawing compass
ruler
wax paper
scissors

push pin
pencil
black marker
modeling clay

PROCEDURE

1. Use the compass to draw a circle with about a 4-inch (10-cm) diameter from the wax paper. Cut out the circle.

2. Stick the pushpin through the center of t.he circle and into the side of the eraser on the pencil.

3. Use the marker to make a black dot on the pencil 112 inch (1.25 cm) inside the edge of the paper circle.

4. Stick a grape-sized piece of clay on the point of the pencil.

5. Rotate the paper circle and observe the position of the black dot.

6. Hold the circle still and rotate the pencil.

RESULTS The black dot always stays between the center of the paper circle and the clay ball, about 1½ inch (1.25 cm) inside the edge of the paper.

WHY? In your model, the paper circle represents the earth and the ball of clay represents the moon. Gravitatlon (mutual attraction between objects) keeps the earth and moon together so that they act as a single body rotating around the sun. Your model uses a pencil to hold the paper earth and the clay moon together. The dot on the pencil represents the center of gravity (balancing point) of our earth-moon system, called the barycenter. The barycenter is the point that maps out the path of the earth-moon system around the sun. The model shows that the barycenter is not a definite place on the surface of the earth, but a point about 2,720 miles (4,352 km) below the earth's surface on the side facing the moon.

BARYCENTER

EARTH

MOON

MOVING TARGET

PURPOSE To simulate aiming a spacecraft for the moon.

MATERIALS scissors   washer
ruler   book
string   paper towel
masking tape

PROCEDURE

1. Cut a 24-inch (60-cm) piece of string.

2. Tape one end of the string to one end of the ruler.

3. Tie the washer to the free end of the string.

4. Place the ruler on a table with about 4 inches (10 cm) of the ruler extending over the edge of the table.

5. Place a book on top of the ruler to secure it to the table.

6. Tear and wad up 10 grape-sized pieces of the paper towel.

7. Pull the hanging washer to the side and release it to start it swinging.

8. Sit about 1 yard (1 m) from the swinging washer.

9. Pitch one wad of paper at a time at the moving washer.

10. Record the number of paper wads that hit the swinging washer.

RESULTS The paper wads hit the washer when aimed at a point in front of the swinging washer.

WHY? It takes time for the paper wads to move through the air. While they move, the washer moves to another position. Astronauts have the same problem when aiming their spacecraft at the moon because the moon, like the washer, is constantly changing positions. The paper wads and the spacecraft must be directed to a point in front of the moving target so that they arrive at the same place at the same time.

ECLIPSE

PURPOSE To demonstrate a solar eclipse.

MATERIALS pen
          poster board
          timer
          helper

PROCEDURE

CAUTION: Never look directly at the sun. It can damage your eyes.

1. 1. Use the pen to draw the largest possible circle on the poster board.

2. 2. Mark an X at one point on the outline of the circle.

3. 3. Place the poster board on the ground in a sunny area outside.

4. 4. Stand in the center of the paper, facing the X. Ask your helper to make a mark on the paper where the center of your shadow crosses the circle.

5. 5. Repeat the previous step every 30 minutes, six or more times during the day.

RESULTS Your shadow crossed the circle at different points during the day.

WHY? A shadow is a dark shape cast upon a surface when something blocks light. You cast a shadow because your body blocks the sun's light. During an eclipse, one object passes through the shadow of another. A solar eclipse occurs when the earth moves into the moon's shadow. At such times, the moon lies between the sun and the earth. The moon's shadow, like your shadow, falls on different areas of the earth because the earth rotates.

DARKER

PURPOSE To determine why some areas of the earth are darker during a solar eclipse.

MATERIALS sheet of printer paper
flashlight
ruler

PROCEDURE

1. Lay the paper on a table.

2. Hold the flashlight about 14 inches (35 cm) from the paper.

3. Place your hand between the light and the paper about 1 inch (2.5 cm) above the paper.

4. Spread your fingers apart.

5. Observe the color of the shadow made by your hand on the paper.

RESULTS The shadow is darker in the center than on the outside.

WHY? Your hand casts a shadow because light traveling in a straight line from the flashlight is blocked by your hand. Light cannot pass through your hand; therefore, a dark shape or shadow appears on the paper. A shadow has two parts-the umbra and the penumbra. The umbra is the dark inner part of a shadow where the light is completely cut off. During a solar eclipse, the umbra of the moon's shadow falls on a small part of the earth. The penumbra is the outer, lighter part of the shadow where the light is only partly cut off. The penumbra of the moon's shadow falls on a larger part of the earth during a solar eclipse.

SUN

PENUMBRA

MOON

UMBRA

EARTH

Darker

BLOCKED

PURPOSE To demonstrate a lunar eclipse.

MATERIALS baseball
flashlight
several books
golf ball

PROCEDURE

1. Place the baseball on a table.

2. Stack some of the books about 12 inches (30 cm) from the baseball.

3. Lay the flashlight on the books and point it toward the baseball. If the light doesn't shine directly on the baseball, raise or lower the flashlight by increasing or decreasing the number and/or size of books used.

4. Hold the golf ball to the side of the baseball.

5. Slowly move the golf ball behind the baseball (the side opposite the flashlight).

RESULTS A dark shadow from the baseball falls across the golf ball as the golf ball moves behind the baseball.

WHY? A lunar eclipse occurs when the moon moves into the earth's shadow. At such times, the earth lies between the sun and the moon. In this experiment, the baseball represents the earth, the flashlight represents the sun, and the golf ball represents the moon. As the moon moves into the shadow of the earth, the part of the moon covered by the shadow is no longer visible. Finally, the entire moon seems to disappear. The reverse happens as the moon moves out of the earth's shadow.

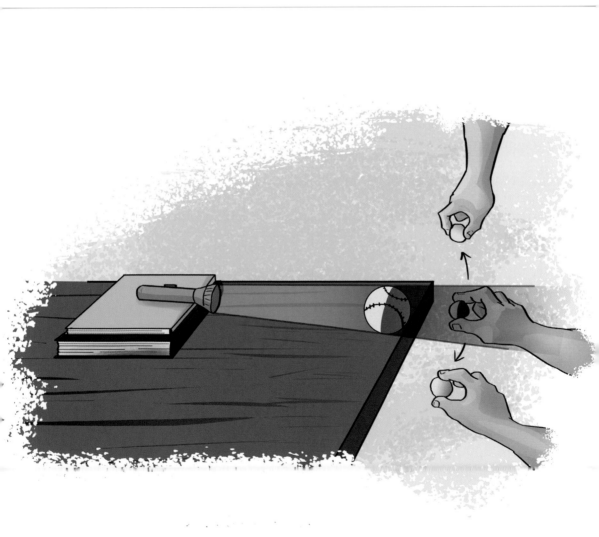

Blocked

WHICH WAY?

PURPOSE To make a shadow compass.

MATERIALS pen
     pencil
           paper
           plate

PROCEDURE

CAUTION: Never look directly at the sun. It can damage your eyes.

1. Use the pen to mark the directions N, S, E, and W on the edge of the paper plate.

2. In the afternoon, lay the paper plate on the ground in a sunny area.

3. Push the point of the pencil through the center of the plate and into the ground about 1 inch (2.5 cm).

4. Move the pencil around until it no longer casts a shadow on the plate.

5. Wait until a shadow appears on the plate, then rotate the plate so that the shadow points toward the letter E.

RESULTS The plate is turned so the letters on the plate point in the general compass directions of north, south, east, and west.

WHY? When you point the end of the pencil straight at the sun, no shadow appears on the paper. The sun appears to move in a general direction from east to west. As it moves toward the west, the sun's light hits the pencil, forming a shadow pointing toward the east. Rotating the plate so that the letter E lines up with the shadow places all the letters in line with the compass directions of north, south, east, and west. Any general direction can then be determined from the shadow compass. (If you had performed the experiment before noon, you would have rotated the plate so that the letter W lined up with the shadow.)

WHERE IS IT?

PURPOSE To determine the position of the sun in the sky.

MATERLALS yardstick (meterstick)
modeling clay
protractor
1-yard (1-m) piece of string
sharpened pencil
helper

PROCEDURE

CAUTION: Never look directly at the sun.

1. Place the measuring stick on an outside table. Point one end toward the sun.

2. Use the clay to stand the protractor upright against the side of the measuring stick, with its center at the end of the stick.

3. Tie one end of the string around the pencil point. Stand the pencil on the measuring stick.

4. Move the pencil back and forth until the shadow of the pencil point strikes the end of the stick.

5. Ask your helper to pull the string to the end of the measuring stick and to read the angle where it crosses the protractor.

6. Repeat steps 4 and 5 at different times.

RESULTS The angle reading varies with the time of day.

Janice VanCleave's Wild, Wacky, and Weird Astronomy Experiments

WHY? Each day the sun appears to rise from below the eastern horizon (a line where the earth and sky appear to meet). It then moves across the sky and sinks below the western horizon. The altitude (height) of the sun changes during the day. At sunrise and sunset, the altitude is zero degrees. Each day the greatest altitude is around noon. During the year, the sun's greatest altitude is during the summer. Its lowest altitude is during the winter.

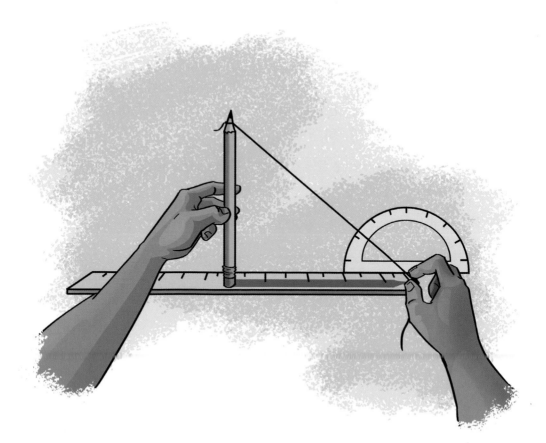

PURPOSE To simulate the magnetic field around spots on the sun.

MATERIALS rubber gloves (the kind used for dishwashing)
scissors
soapless steel wool pad (purchase at a variety store in the paint section)
1-teaspoon (5-ml) measuring spoon
small round magnet
sheet of typing paper

PROCEDURE

1. Put on the gloves and use the scissors to cut very tiny pieces from the steel wool pad. The smaller the pieces, the better. Cut enough pieces to fill the measuring spoon.

CAUTION: Do not remove the gloves. They prevent the steel wool from damaging your skin.

2. Place the magnet on a wooden table and cover it with the paper.

3. Sprinkle the steel wool pieces on the paper above the magnet.

RESULTS The steel wool pieces form a pattern on the paper above the magnet.

WHY? A magnetic field is the area around a magnet in which the force of the magnet affects the movement of other magnetic objects, such as steel wool. This area is made up of invisible lines of magnetic force. The small pieces of steel wool follow the lines of force, allowing you to "see" the magnetic field. Magnetic fields exist on the sun. Dark spots on the sun where gases are cooler are called sunspots. Like magnets, the sunspots are surrounded by magnetic fields that attract magnetic materials.

DIRECT

PURPOSE To determine why Mars and the earth both have cold poles.

MATERIALS book

            masking tape

            2 sheets of black construction paper

            2 thermometers

PROCEDURE

1. Place the book on a flat surface in the sun.

2. Tape one piece of black paper on each side of the book.

3. Turn the book so that one sheet of paper receives direct sunlight.

4. Tape a thermometer on top of each sheet of black paper.

5. Read the temperature on both thermometers after 10 minutes.

RESULTS The thermometer facing the sun has a higher temperature.

WHY? The black paper facing the sun receives more direct rays of sunlight than the sheet on the opposite side of the book. Areas that receive direct light rays from the sun are much hotter. The earth's equator receives about 2112 times as much heat during the year as does the area around the poles. Mars, like the earth, has colder pole areas. Both of these planets are slightly tilted in their relationship to the sun, causing the center to receive more direct solar light rays than do the poles.

SLANTING RAYS

DIRECT RAYS

SUN SIZE

PURPOSE To calculate the diameter of the sun.

MATERIALS pencil straight pin
           choot of typing papor macking tape
           metric ruler meterstick
           index card adult helper

PROCEDURE

CAUTION: Never look directly at the sun.

1. Use the ruler to draw two parallel lines 2 mm apart on the sheet of paper.

2. Ask an adult to punch a hole in the center of the index card with the pin.

3. Fold over 1 cm of one short end of the index card. Tape the folded edge to the zero end of the meterstick.

4. Stand the meterstick outside in a sunny area and hold the sheet of paper at the 218-mm mark.

5. Adjust the stick and paper so that the shadow of the card falls on the paper and the circle of light fills the space between the lines you drew.

RESULTS The circle of light fits between the lines. Thus, it has a 2-mm diameter.

WHY? The distance from the hole in the card to the paper (218 mm) divided by the diameter of the circle (2 mm) equals 109. Thus, the distance of 218 mm divided by 109 equals the diameter of the circle. Astronomers have determined that an approximate diameter of the sun can also be calculated by dividing the distance from the sun to the earth (150,000,000 km) by 109. Thus, the diameter of the sun is about 1,376,147 km.

MOONBEAMS

PURPOSE To compare your speed to the speed of moonlight.

MATERIALS 2 pencils
stopwatch
yardstick (meterstick)
2 helpers

PROCEDURE

1. Lay one of the pencils on the ground to mark a starting line.

2. Have a trial run to determine about how far you can run in 4 seconds. Stand at the starting line. Ask one helper, called the "marking helper," to stand to the side and about 7 yards (6.4 m) in front of the starting line.

3. When your second helper, called the "timer;" says "Start," run forward as fast as you can.

4. When the timer says "Stop" (at the end of 4 seconds), the marking helper lays a pencil at your location, and you stop as soon as possible.

5. Rest, then have a real run by repeating steps 2 through 4.

6. Use the measuring stick to measure the distance. Round the distance to the nearest yard (meter).

7. Divide the distance by 3.

RESULTS Dividing the distance you traveled by 3 tells you the distance you traveled in one-third the time, or 1 ⅓ seconds. The result tor the author of this book was 7 yards (6.4 m) in 1113 seconds.

WHY? 1⅓ seconds is the length of time it takes for light to travel from the moon to the earth. The author of this book raced across her yard at a speed of 7 yards (6.4 m) in 1⅓ seconds while moonbeams of light traveled about 420,000,000 yards (384,000,000 m) to the earth in the same amount of time.

SHINER

PURPOSE To demonstrate why the moon shines.

MATERIALS bicycle reflector
flashlight

PROCEDURE

1. Do this experiment at night.

2. Point the flashlight at the bicycle reflector.

3. Turn the flashlight off.

RESULTS The reflector glows only when the flashlight is on.

WHY? The flashlight is luminous (gives off its own light). The reflector is not luminous, meaning it does not give off its own light. It is designed to reflect light from other sources in different directions. The mopn, like the reflector, is not luminous. The moon reflects light from the sun. Without the sun, there would be no moonlight.

Shiner

HEAVY

PURPOSE To simulate the effect of the moon's gravity on weight.

MATERIALS 24-inch (60-cm) piece of string
rock, about the size of a small apple
rubber band
large cooking pot or bucket
tap water

PROCEDURE

1. Tie one end of the string around the rock and attach the other end of the string to the rubber band.

2. Place the pot on a table and set the rock inside.

3. Hold the free end of the rubber band and gently lift the rock just above the bottom of the pot.

4. Observe the length of the rubber band.

5. Fill the pot with water and repeat steps 3 and 4.

RESULTS The rubber band stretched less when the rock was raised in water.

WHY? Gravity (force that pulls toward the center of the earth) pulls the rock down, causing the attached rubber band to stretch. But when water is added to the pot, the water pushes up on the rock, canceling some of the downward pull of gravity. Raising the rock in the water simulates the effect of the moon's gravity on weight. The moon's gravity is only one-sixth as strong as the gravity on the earth.

Janice VanCleave's Wild, Wacky, and Weird Astronomy Experiments

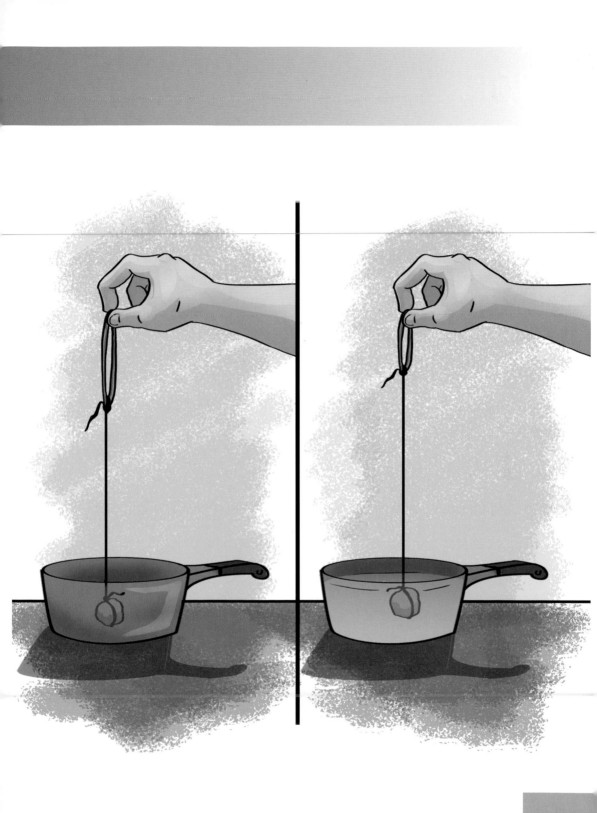

Heavy

PLOP!

PURPOSE To determine the type of surface where craters are best formed.

MATERIALS 8-inch (20-cm) square of aluminum foil
newspaper
1 golf ball-sized rock
carpeted floor
uncarpeted floor

PROCEDURE

1. Lay the newspaper on the carpet.

2. Lay one foil square on top of the newspaper.

3. Stand at the edge of the foil.

4. Hold the rock waist high and drop it in the center of the foil.

5. Repeat steps 1 through 4 on an uncarpeted, hard floor.

6. Examine both pieces of foil.

RESULTS The rock made a larger impression on the foil lying on the soft carpet.

WHY? The rock sank into the softer carpet surface, which allowed more of the ball to be pressed against the paper. Like the rock, a meteorite (a stony or metallic object from space that falls through an atmosphere and strikes the surface of a celestial body) makes a larger imprint when it strikes a soft surface. Bowl-shaped holes called craters are best formed when meteorites strike soft, powdery surfaces such as the surface of the moon.

Plop!

SPLATTER

PURPOSE To determine why moon craters are spread out.

MATERIALS 2 cups (500 ml) soil
2-quart (2-liter) bowl
tap water

spoon
plate
4-6 pebbles

PROCEDURE

1. Pour the soil into the bowl. Add small amounts of water, stirring continuously, until a muddy mixture forms.

2. Fill the plate with the mud mixture. Shake the plate to smooth out the surface of the mud.

3. Drop each pebble, one at a time, from a height of about 24 inches (60 cm) above the plate.

4. Move your hand so that the pebbles hit different areas of the mud's surface.

RESULTS Each pebble produces a splatter of liquid and craterlike indentations on the surface.

WHY? The falling pebbles simulate meteorites. The tremendous amount of heat produced by the impact of large meteorites melts the surface, and the liquid surface splatters, as did the mud. The decreased gravity on the moon allows the liquid to be blown higher and over a larger area. Thus the rims of many of the craters on the moon overlap, and the craters are separated by rough areas where thin layers of the liquid have fallen on the surface.

Too Much

PURPOSE To determine why the moon's daytime temperature is so high.

MATERIALS sheet of black construction paper
desk lamp
2 thermometers
timer

PROCEDURE

1. Lay the paper under the lamp.

2. Place one thermometer on the paper and position the lamp about 4 inches (10 cm) from its bulb.

3. Place the second thermometer away from the lamp.

4. Turn on the lamp and record both temperatures after 5 minutes.

RESULTS The reading on the thermometer under the lamp is much higher than on the other thermometer.

WHY? The moon's daytime temperature is about 266 degrees Fahrenheit (130°C). This is because the sun shines on the moon's surface continuously for about two earth weeks. There is also very little protection from the solar rays because the moon's gravity is so weak that a protective atmosphere cannot be captured as it is around the earth. Therefore, the sun heats the surface to temperatures above the boiling point of water. While the sunny side is cooking, like the thermometer under the lamp, the shaded side is exposed to very cold space. (The second thermometer is not exposed to the cold, but it is cooler.) The shady side of the moon cools to about -279.4°F (-173°C).

Too Much

BRIGHTEST STAR

PURPOSE To locate the brightest star.

MATERIALS compass

clear sky

PROCEDURE

CAUTION: Never look directly at the sun.

1. Just before sunrise, go outside and find a good view of the sky above the horizon.

2. Use the compass to determine the directions of east and west.

3. Face the east and look for a very bright star in the sky above the horizon.

4. If you don't see the star at sunrise, look for it above the western horizon after sunset.

RESULTS What appears to be a very bright star is usually seen in the morning before sunrise or in the evening after sunset. Sometimes the star is not visible.

WHY? The brightest star in the sky is not really a star, but the planet Venus. It appears as a bright star because the dense, unbroken clouds surrounding the planet reflect about 75 percent of the incoming sunlight back into space. The movement of the planet around the sun, as seen from the earth, makes it appear as an "evening" or "morning" star. It appears in the evening in the western sky when moving toward the earth.

It is in the eastern sky in the morning after it has passed between the sun and the earth and begins moving away from the earth. If the star is too close to the sun, the brightness of the sun blocks out the light from Venus and it cannot be seen.

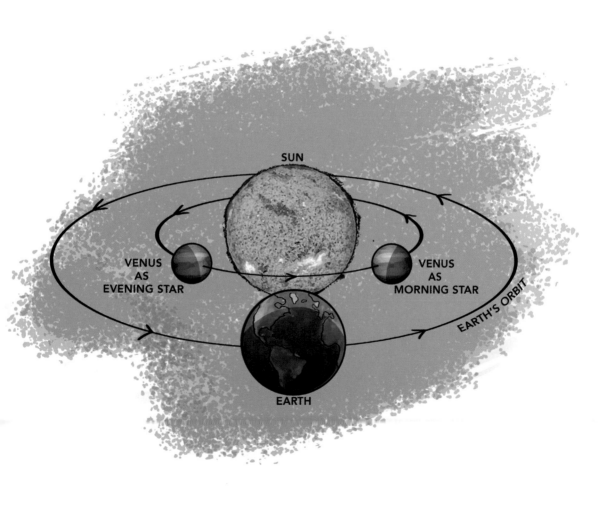

TWINKLING STAR

PURPOSE To simulate twinkling stars.

MATERIALS 12-by-12-inch (30-by-30-cm) square of aluminum foil
2-quart (2-liter) glass bowl
tap water
flashlight
pencil

PROCEDURE

1. Crumple the foil with your hands. Open up the crumpled foil and place it on a table.

2. Fill the bowl with water and place it on top of the foil.

3. Darken the room and hold the flashlight about 12 inches (30 cm) above the bowl.

4. Gently tap the surface of the water with the pencil.

5. Observe the foil through the moving water.

RESULTS Light reflecting from the foil appears to twinkle.

WHY? The up-and-down movement of the water causes the depth of the water to vary. Light rays reflecting from the foil twinkle because they refract, or bend, differently as they pass through different depths of water. To an observer on earth, light rays from distant stars appear to twinkle because they also refract differently as they move through different thicknesses of air in the earth's atmosphere. This twinkling or motion of starlight is called scintillation.

Twinkling Star

Star Projector

PURPOSE To make a star projector.

MATERIALS round box, such as an empty oatmeal box
drawing compass
sheet of black construction paper
scissors
rubber band
chalk
flashlight
adult helper

PROCEDURE

1. Ask an adult to remove both ends of the box.

2. Use the compass to draw a circle on the paper 2 inches (5 cm) wider than the end of the box.

3. Cut out the circle and place it over one end of the box. Secure the paper with the rubber band.

4. Use the chalk to draw the star pattern on the paper cover.

5. With the pointed end of the compass, make a hole through each star on the paper cover.

6. Place the flashlight inside the box. Darken the room and turn on the flashlight.

7. Turn the side of the box with the paper toward the ceiling. Move the flashlight back and forth in the box until a clear image of light spots appears on the ceiling.

RESULTS An enlarged pattern of the holes in the paper are projected onto the ceiling.

WHY? Light shining through the holes spreads out, producing larger circles of light on the ceiling. The stars projected on the ceiling are in the correct order as seen in the sky. The star pattern   is the constellation (grouping of stars) called Draco.

STAR
PATTERN

OATS

PURPOSE To demonstrate how a refracting telescope works.

MATERIALS 2 magnifying lenses
        sheet of notebook paper

CAUTION: Never look at the sun through a magnifying lens. You will damage your eyes. Never point the lens at the sun.

PROCEDURE

1. In a darkened room, close one eye and look at an open window through one of the magnifying lenses.

2. Move the lens back and forth slowly until the objects outside the window are clearly in focus.

3. Without moving the lens, place the paper between you and the lens.

4. Move the paper back and forth until a clear image appears on the sheet.

5. Replace the paper with the second lens.

6. Move the second lens back and forth to find the position where the image looks clear when looking through both lenses.

RESULTS A small, inverted image of the objects outside the window is projected onto the paper. This image is larger when seen through both lenses.

WHY? A refracting telescope has two lenses, an objective lens (the lens closer to the object being viewed) and an eyepiece (the lens closer to your eye). The two magnifying lenses in this activity represent the objective lens and eyepiece in a refracting telescope. The objective lens collects light from distant objects and brings it into focus in front of the eyepiece. This image can be projected onto a screen, such as the paper. When you look through the magnifying lens eyepiece or a real eyepiece in a telescope, you see the same image, but it is magnified.

GLOSSARY

ALTITUDE Height.

BARYCENTER The center of gravity point between the earth-moon system, which maps out the path of the earth moon system around the sun.

CELESTIAL Of the heavens or sky.

CENTER OF GRAVITY The point at which an object balances.

CONDUCTOR A material that allows electricity, heat, or sound to move through it.

CONSTELLATION A group of stars that, viewed from the earth, form the outline of an object or figure.

CRATER A bowl-shaped depression.

ECLIPSE When one object passes in front of another object and thus blocks the light from that object.

GRAVITATION The mutual attraction between objects.

GRAVITY A force that pulls toward the center of a celestial body, such as the earth.

LUMINOUS Giving off its own light.

MAGNETIC FIELD The area around a magnet in which the force of the magnet affects the movement of other magnetic objects; made up of invisible lines of magnetic force.

METEORITE A stony or metallic object from space that falls through an atmosphere and strikes the surface of a celestial body.

MIRAGE An optical illusion due to atmospheric conditions.

ORBIT The path of an object around another body; planets moving around the sun.

PENUMBRA The outer, lighter part of a shadow.

REFRACT To bend.

SATELLITE A small body moving around a larger body.

SCINTILLATION The twinkling or motion of starlight.

SOLAR ECLIPSE The event resulting when the moon passes in front of the sun and casts a shadow onto parts of the earth.

FOR MORE INFORMATION

American Astronomical Society
  2000 Florida Ave., NW, Suite 300
  Washington, DC 20009-1231, USA
  (202) 328-2010
  website: http://aas.org
  The AAS is the major organization of professional astronomers in North
  America. Locate an observatory near you, find out about Astronomy
  Ambassadors, and learn about the latest news in astronomy.

National Aeronautics and Space Administration (NASA)
  NASA Headquarters
  300 E. Street SW, Suite 5R30
  Washington, DC 20546
  (202) 358-0001
  website: http://www.nasa.gov
  NASA is the premier organization for all things space! Join the NASA
  Kids' Club, learn about the International Space Station and historic space
  missions, view solar system photographs, and learn more about space
  technology.

National Science Foundation (NSF)
  4201 Wilson Boulevard
  Arlington, Virginia 22230, USA
  (703) 292-5111
  website: http://www.nsf.gov/
  The NSF is dedicated to science, engineering, education. Learn how to
  be a Citizen Scientist, read about the latest scientific discoveries, and
  discover the newest innovations in technology.

The Royal Astronomical Society of Canada
  203-4920 Dundas Street West
  Toronto ON M9A 1B7
  Canada
  website: http://rasc.ca
  The Royal Astronomical Society of Canada provides many educational
  resources, including Ask an Astronomer, observation calendars, photographs, and public astronomy events.

The Society for Science and the Public
  Student Science
  1719 N Street, N.W.
  Washington, D.C. 20036
  (800) 552-4412
  website: https://student.societyforscience.org
  The Society for Science and the Public presents many science project
  resources, such as science news for students, the latest updates on the
  Intel Science Talent Search and the Intel International Science and Engineering Fair, and information about cool jobs and doing science.

WEBSITES

Because of the changing nature of Internet links, Rosen Publishing has
developed an online list of websites related to the subject of this book. This
site is updated regularly. Please use this link to access this list:

http://www.rosenlinks.com/JVCW/astro

FOR FURTHER READING

Ardley, Neil. *101 Great Science Experiments*. New York: DK Ltd., 2014.

Buczynski, Sandy. *Designing a Winning Science Fair Project* (Information Explorer Junior). Ann Arbor, MI: Cherry Lake Publishing, 2014.

Datnow, Claire. *Edwin Hubble: Genius Discoverer of Galaxies* (Genius Scientists and their Genius Ideas). Berkeley Heights, NJ: Enslow Publishers, Inc., 2015.

Henneberg, Susan. *Creating Science Fair Projects with Cool New Digital Tools* (Way Beyond PowerPoint: Making 21st Century Presentations). New York: Rosen Central, 2014.

Kawa, Katie. *Freaky Space Stories* (Freaky True Science). New York: Gareth Stevens Publishing, 2016.

Kuskowski, Alex. *Stargazing* (Out of this World). Minneapolis: Super Sandcastle, 2016.

Levy, Joel. *The Universe Explained* (Guide for Curious Minds). New York: Rosen Publishing, 2014.

Margles, Samantha. *Mythbusters Science Fair Book*. New York: Scholastic, 2011.

McGill, Jordan. *Space Science Fair Projects* (Science Fair Projects). New York: AV2 by Weigl, 2012.

Riggs, Kate. *Moons* (Across the Universe). Mankato, Minn: Creative Education/Creative Paperbacks, 2015.

Rockett, Paul. *70 Thousand Million, Million, Million Stars in Space* (The Big

Countdown). Chicago: Capstone Raintree, 2016.

Saucier, C. A. P. *Explore the Cosmos Like Neil DeGrasse Tyson: A Space Science Journey*. Amherst, NY: Prometheus Books, 2015.

Spilsbury, Louise. *Space* (Make and Learn). New York: PowerKids Press, 2015.

INDEX

moonlight, speed of, 36–37
"morning" star, 48
moving target, 18–19

N
Neptune, 14–15

O
orbital body, outermost, 14

P
penumbra, 22
Pluto, 15
point of balance, 16–17
poles, cold, 32–33

R
refracting telescope, 54–55

S
satellites, shepherd, 13
Saturn's rings, 12–13
scientific method, 6–7
scintillation, 51
shadow, 20–21, 22
shadow compass, 26–27
shepherd satellites, 13
sky gazer, 54–55
solar eclipse, 20–21, 22–23

space, 11
spacecraft, aiming at the moon, 18–19
splatters, understanding moon craters, 44–45
spots, sun, 30–31
star
    brightest, 48–49
    "evening", 48
    "morning", 48
star projector, 52–53
stars, twinkling, 50–51
sun, altitude of, 29
sun, diameter of, 34–35
sun, the, position of, 28–29
sunspots, 30–31

T
telescope, refracting, 54–55
temperature, daylight, of the moon, 46–47
twinkling stars, 50–51

U
umbra, 22

V
vacuum, 11
Venus, 9, 48, 49

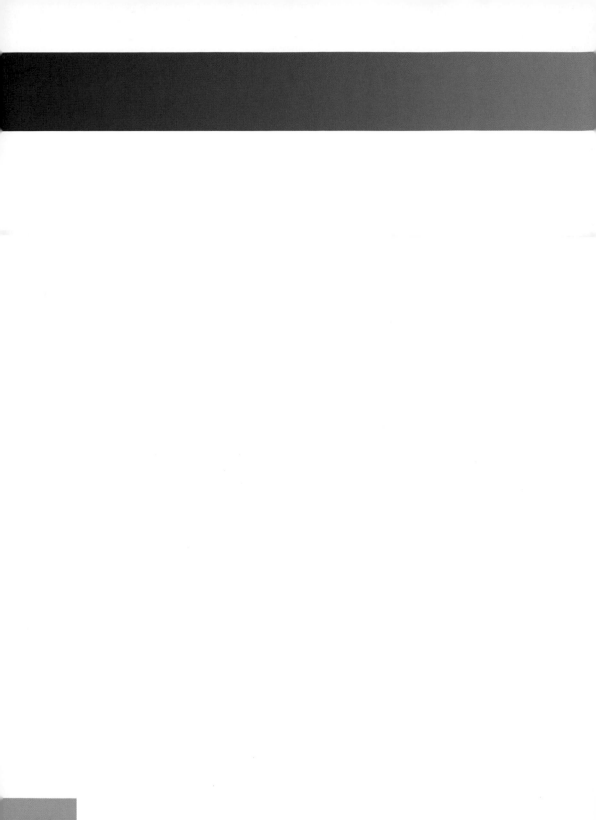

Janice VanCleave's Wild, Wacky, and Weird Astronomy Experiments